ANTIQUIS PATRIBUS
QUI NOS INTACTA
TRADIDERUNT
SANCTA LITURGIA
HOC
PIETATIS OPUS,
QUAMVIS PARVULUM,
AMANTER
DEDICO

THE SACRED LITURGY

THE SACRED LITURGY

by a Benedictine monk

The Saint Austin Press
MCMXCIX

THE SAINT AUSTIN PRESS
296 Brockley Road
London   SE4 2RA
Tel   +44 (0) 181 692 6009
Fax +44 (0) 181 469 3609

Email: books@saintaustin.org
http://www.saintaustin.org

From the original French:
La Sainte Liturgie, 1982, Éditions Sainte Madeleine

English edition © 1999, The Saint Austin Press

A catalogue record for this book is available from the British
Library.

ISBN 1 901157 07 5

Designed and printed by NEWTON Design & Print

Table of Contents

Introduction 13

The Temple of Creation 17
A theology of images 19
A liturgy in tune with the universe 24
Prayer and poetry 26

The Approach to the Heavenly Temple 31
The coming of joy 33
The heavenly sacrifice 38
The angels in our midst .42

Man and Rite 47
The patrimony of mankind 49
An unfathomable mystery 53
The benign influence of the liturgy 55
The primacy of contemplation 56
The sense of the Church 59
The feeling for beauty 62
The love of rule and order 65
The sweet attraction of heavenly things 68

EPILOGUE - Addresses to novices 77
The prayer of the day 79
The whole of our existence is a liturgical action 93

The Sacred Liturgy

"For behold, as soon as the voice of thy salutation sounded in my ears, the infant in my womb leaped for joy."

(Luke i.44)

THREE unceasing miracles are found in the garden of the Bride of Christ: the wisdom of her doctors, the heroism of her saints, and the splendour of her Liturgy. *Et hi tres unum sunt!* These three things are one because the Liturgy is itself a song of wisdom and of love: it brings together the two orders of intelligence and love and directs them upwards in prayer.

It is not surprising, then, that when we see and hear the Church's liturgy, be it the chanting of the

Office or the administration of the sacraments, we see in it the secret of our destiny; and we feel that leaping for joy in our whole being that St John the Baptist felt at Mary's salutation. The voice of the Bride ravishes the heart of the Bridegroom and sanctifies the souls of her children, and so the Church fulfills the double role of praising God and sanctifying souls. Admittedly this leaping for joy cannot be for each of us what it was for John the Baptist, the sign of a sudden and entire transformation which made him the greatest among the sons of women; but we can be moved by the action of the liturgy so as to feel that salvation is proclaimed and that we are being offered a foretaste of eternal life; and little by little this will transform us. And if it happens that we hear the accents of another world carried in the sounds of a sacral language heard within one of those temples of stone our fathers built so well and which are so full of the spirit of prayer, then we may come to that mysterious point where gestures and words make up a kind of divine harmony, a distant echo of the songs of the celestial city, songs which are alone capable of drawing our attention a little away from the things of earth.

"I am always shaken by the grandeur of the ceremonies of the Church," said St Teresa of Avila. If we ask ourselves what is the secret of this grandeur, we will see that it comes much less from the shape and size our human contribution can give it than from some essential liturgical reality drawing upon two very distinct orders of grandeur: the cosmic grandeur of our created universe and the supernatural grandeur of the Kingdom of Heaven.

The Temple of Creation

FOR some years now the splendid scholarly study of the writings of the Fathers of the Church has allowed us to understand better how even the least important ceremony contracts the span of time and gathers into itself the whole history of salvation: Genesis, Exodus, the books of the prophets, all culminating in the mystery which is Christ; even a minor ceremony will announce and make present the Kingdom of God once and for all fulfilled, *when God will be all in all.*

Reading the Fathers, especially St Clement of Alexandria, St Maximus and St Augustine one cannot help but notice how far the liturgy of the Church keeps time with the rhythm of the universe, the created universe itself being a temple of praise within which an endless liturgy unfolds. These great Fathers of the Church were concerned not only with the twelve articles of the creed; they teach us also to look at the world itself with the eyes of faith, as the shining garment of Almighty God himself and to look at the succession of the days as the unrolling of a sacred pageant.

Is there not perhaps in our created universe a vast liturgical action sketched out for us, a strange theatre of sounds and signs waiting for man himself to give it some fully formed significance? Perhaps one may see in the unbelievable abundance of natural forms and rhythms, in all the different realms of existence - in their hierarchic order, beginning deep in matter and rising to where the spirit is enthroned - perhaps one may see here St Paul's tense expectation of the whole of creation groaning in the labour of birth.[1] It is almost as though this great *theatrum mundi* awaits one who will lead its chorus of praise. For St Maximus the universe was like "a cosmic church, where the nave was the sensible world and the choir the spiritual world." St

Augustine had the same ample thought: *"Universi saeculi pulchritudo velut magnum carmen ineffabilis modulatoris* - the beauty of the whole of creation is like a great poem created by some incomparable master,"* as he says in his commentary on the psalms. Let us follow him in this train of thought.

A theology of images

The animal and vegetable kingdoms with their abundance of different life-forms, the alternation of the seasons, the rhythm of the hours marked by the sun, the exact circling of the stars, all of this makes up a silent, expectant liturgy. It is an image that pleases God because his mark is upon it, the light of his word. The world is full of traces and likenesses of God. The creation is an image of the creator, an innocent image, not tarnished, but not yet glorified. How can one not see that the light of the sun is as new a thing this day as when its rays first shone upon the surface of the earth in the dawn of creation? How can one not see that the air we breathe is as virginal a thing as that full breath of air breathed in by the first man as he awoke to life?

This never changing newness of created things in their pristine purity is the great miracle of existence. Few human beings are aware of it, but nevertheless with the exception of the supernatural order of things it is the most lucid expression of the divine within the created universe. And it is this that allows us to take seriously the Augustinian idea of the world as a poem written by God.

We find in the prologue to St John's Gospel a phrase that explains very well God's giving of light to his creation. St Augustine, in fact, punctuates the text in a way that emphasizes the significance of this act. Here are St John's words as we find them in the missal: *"Omnia per ipsum facta sunt: et sine ipso factum est nihil quod factum est: in ipso vita erat, et vita erat lux hominum."* [2] Here is the punctuation adopted by St Augustine (we know that in the original manuscripts there is no punctuation): *"Omnia per ipsum facta sunt et sine ipso facta est nihil."* (Then a new sentence.) *"Quod factum est in ipso vita erat."* We may translate: "All things were made by Him and without Him was nothing made. What was made in Him was life."

In St Augustine's commentary on this text we find an idea of great beauty and nobility: everything that lives has life because it is held unceasingly in the mind of God, no matter how more or less humble its terrestrial state:

"As well as I can, here is how I would explain the matter. A joiner makes a cabinet *(faber facit*

20

arcum). He begins by having the cabinet as an idea in his mind (*in arte*). The cabinet of course does not exist in his mind in the same way that it exists when it becomes visible to the eye. In the idea it exists invisibly; once made it exists visibly. So now the cabinet has been made: does it for that reason cease to exist in the idea?... Now let us make a distinction: the cabinet as it exists in reality is not a living thing, but in the idea it is a living thing because the soul of the workman is living and that living soul has encompassed the whole of the work to be done before producing it in the outside world. In the same way, my dear brethren, the Wisdom of God by which all things were made encompassed within itself the idea of all those beings before creating them. You see the earth; well, there is also an earth in God's idea of it. You see the sun and the moon; well, they too exist as ideas. But in their external reality they are inanimate bodies whereas in the divine ideas of them they live: *in arte vita sunt.*" (Tract. In Jo. I, 17.)

Remember that expression: *in arte*. The *ars* is the plan of execution, the guiding idea. St Bonaventure is thinking in Augustinian terms when he says that the word is the art (*ars*) of the Father. This is as much as to say that the created universe is a thought in act, a signature, a concrete realised image emanating from the divine Thought. This is why when in his prologue St

21

John continues: "*et vita erat lux hominum,*" the continuity is from Him who links together life and light. What was made in Him was life and this life was the light of men.

This is so much as to say that we are illumined by the same divine light which brought into visible being the *magnum carmen*, "the poem of creation the work of an incomparable artist." And this light speaks to us of God: "*In lumine tuo videbimus lumen*". It is in your light that we shall see light as the Psalmist says in Psalm 35. In your light, that is to say that creative light which Denis Areopagite calls "*Autokallopoios*" (of itself productive of all beauty) and which St Augustine calls wisdom or art. It is in this divine Light and in this alone that we are able to see the true reality of created things, the sacred chant of their being and the mystery of their vocation!

How should we not see in this great work of creation, its harmony ever new and fresh, a kind of natural song of praise, a cosmic liturgy rising up to God? This idea which was later to come to fruition in Franciscan theology seems to accord with all that is most essentially Catholic; its doctrinal roots are found in the Greek Fathers, for whom there was no created good, even natural good, which is not to be conceived of as a reflection of, and participation in, the light of the Word. *Mimesis* (imitation) and *methexis* (participation) are words encountered constantly in their writings.

It is in this spirit that we should read the great work by Denis the Areopagite called the *Celestial Hierarchy*. Denis' whole doctrine can be summed up in three key words: image, outpouring, participation. According to him everything comes to us by means of the illumination of the "principle light" (*Archiphotos*) which "descends with loving kindness and in many different ways towards the objects of its providence to draw us back to the One, back to the radical, deifying simplicity of the Father who is all in all." In this descent of light and in the ascending reflux of beings illumined and placed in hierarchical order by the Word, splendour of the Father, the whole universe climbs towards its central principle in an awesome celebration in which the human creature also finds its part. "We ourselves," writes St Maximus the Confessor, "in the unfolding pageant of our present lives, are first engendered like any other earthly animal, then we become children, then we are carried along from infancy to the wrinkled skin of age, like a flower that lasts an instant of time, then dying to at last pass into another life - we are truly to be called a game played by God." (*Mystagogy*) We find the same idea in St Clement of Alexandria, for whom the Word is essentially He who "has ordered all things by measure, having brought the dissonance of separate elements to the discipline of accord, to make the world for himself a single symphony of sound." *(Protrepticos)*

But this symphony, compromised by sin and by the fall of man, is in its turn grasped and purified by the great sweeping movement of the redemptive action of the Son of God. The incarnate Word is not only King of the nations of the earth; He has sovereignty over the whole universe, and creation itself acquires a new dignity from the moment the earth is made literally his footstool - *scabellum pedum tuorum* - and from the moment when the stream of blood from the crucified Christ bathes it in the river of His love. A famous Passion hymn puts it memorably:

> *Mite corpus perforatur*
> *Sanguis, unda profluit:*
> *Terra, pontus, astra, mundus*
> *Quo lavantur flumine!* [3]

A liturgy in tune with the universe

It will hardly seem surprising, in the light of this doctrine, that the celebration of the Christian Liturgy, taking place as it does within our churches, but in tune with the rhythms of the universe beyond, has more life-breath and more vigour, the more it derives the natural elements of its poetry and its sacraments from the blind and luminous world that surrounds it.

The liturgical cycle of the Church keeps step with the changing of the seasons in their yearly round, as they form a crown of blessings, in the words of Psalm 64, from the bounteous hand of God. Let us see how the liturgical round keeps step with the cycle of the seasons. Christmas, the Mystery of the royal birth of the Son of God, corresponds to the winter solstice, which is the point at which the sun begins its victorious march in a movement of steady growth, with the darkness retreating at the advance of light. Easter, on the other hand, corresponds to the new growth of spring; it is well described in the *Salva festa dies*: "The beauty of the reborn world bears witness that the whole of creation comes back to life with its Lord. After a melancholy sojourn in the underworld, everywhere the woods are bursting into leaf and the fields are blossoming with flowers."

And so the Church, successor to the first ages of mankind when the pact was sealed between man and the created world, has not expelled from her heart the old pagan loves. She has not lost the savour of earth and sun, she has only purified them; as she has purified her alliance with Ceres and Demeter - goddesses of the harvest and of fruitful fields - by using bread, wine and oil in the confection of her sacraments, so she structures her Divine Office to follow the movements of the sun in the sky.

Prayer and poetry

On each day of the week at Vespers, the hymns of the Roman breviary tell of a phase in the history of creation, while the Lauds hymns sing of the light of day dissipating the darkness of night. With consummate art the liturgy takes us from the plane of created light to that of the eternal light. Each morning the dawn puts darkness to flight, as Christ the light of the world puts to flight the darkness of sin. The poetry of the liturgy sheds the light of hope upon everyday life with an undreamed of freshness of invention. So it is with a famous hymn for the Sundays of winter, where each stanza begins with the crowing of the cock:

> *At cock crow hope is born again,*
> *The sick take heart again for life,*
> *The sailor feels new courage in the storm,*
> *The brigand sheathes his sword.*

The chanting of the psalms, which forms the main framework of liturgical prayer, ripples with images that make up a body of poetry of powerful and primal energy that would be difficult to match elsewhere. Here is how the psalmist speaks of God:

"The Lord is clothed with light as with a cloak. He touches the mountains and they smoke. He is seen in the

thunder and he marches on the wings of the wind. He wakes like a warrior overcome with wine. Before him the rivers clap their hands. The hills exult, they leap like rams, and the small hills like lambs."[4]

There is always an image or a resonant word which can catch and feed one's imagination.

The liturgy of the Church is not just in tune with natural time: it redeems time. Immersed with joy in the great flood of creatures from which it derives its abundance of images, the liturgy transfigures this created order and prepares it for its ultimate transformation. From wine, the natural drink that makes glad the heart of man, the Church makes a royal vintage that envelopes the world in its purple, rehabilitates it and consecrates it with an even more solemn consecration than that of the first day of creation.

Louis Veuillot, the famous French catholic writer once wrote these words on the occasion of the consecration of a church:

"Oil, water, wine, fire, ashes, salt, wax, hyssop, gold, silver, stone, lime, sand, all belong to the Church and she makes sovereign use of them. The church comes to make all well, to save all things, to unite them together. Sin has destroyed the harmony between God and man, and between man and the created world." And Veuillot rightly concludes that: "paganism sullied the natural

27

order, Protestantism rejects it, the Church consecrates it."[5]

The rite of the consecration - or dedication - of a church is the most sumptuous of all the liturgical ceremonies, full of the most splendid lyrical incantations. Two prayers in particular express the mystery of the cosmic order illumined by the divine presence. Here is the prayer of the blessing of the lime and sand:

"Almighty God, you who conserve all things high and low in the scale of being, you who encompass all creatures and who are found at the centre of their being, sanctify this lime and this sand which you have created."

And the great Preface sung outside the church, at the main door, is in the same terms:

"O holy and blessed Trinity, purifying all, cleansing all, beautifying all things: O blessed majesty of God, filling all, encompassing all, disposing all things: O hand of God, holy and blessed, which sanctifies and enriches all things..."

The Church consecrates the world in order to offer it to God and in the act of offering it, she sanctifies and divinises it. And from where does the power of the liturgy over our universe come if not from a profound complicity with the world of signs and symbols? It is the whole art of the liturgy to make a reality of the wish once expressed by Charles Péguy "that a holiness

28

should arise from the earth." The liturgy directs up to God the song of His creatures. It has within it just what is needed of the earth to make it possible to translate the realities of Heaven into image and symbol. Among the jewels offered to the Bride of Christ by the sweet kingdom of earth, there is poetry, a presence in the liturgy of something deriving from the secular world, rather as the Israelites brought with them to the Promised Land something of the treasures of Egypt. It is no small matter that the liturgy brings with it something of the treasures of earth, that in some way it renders into human language the inexpressible groaning of the Spirit of God which is the ground of all prayer, blended with the numberless voices of creation. Baudelaire in a famous poem called *les Phares* ('Beacons'), where he speaks of the creative energy of art through the ages, celebrates this constant murmuring of art and poetry arising in the liturgy to God:

For it is truly, O Lord, the best witness to our own human dignity, this quiet ardour of sound arising age after age to die away at the very edge of your eternity.

The Approach to the Heavenly Temple

E who, like
the Ephesians to whom St Paul wrote in the year
60 or 62 A.D., are no longer *strangers and foreigners
but fellow citizens with the saints,* desire more than all
the treasures of the earth, the grace which the
Church pours out upon her children when she
raises them from temporal things to give them a
foretaste of the joys of eternity. The stream of
the liturgy, and this is its merit, gathers up the
treasures of the earth and flows with them into
the great ocean of divine life. At the threshold of

the sanctuary the images and signs derived from temporal things cease and what passes into the sanctuary is the human soul in the naked act of prayer, allowing the signs to pass away so that it should be filled with the fullness of God. As we read in the Apocalypse, the elect shall need no lamps because the lord Himself is their light.

If we ask how it is that those who take their part in the drama of the liturgy are led along the path to their homeland and to what degree they can approach the *beauty that is beyond speech*[6] then we must answer that the upward way has about it a double aspect. Creation itself furnishes us with an abundance of images and symbols and these go to make up the way, but there must also be a sense of a goal to be pursued, that actual desire to pass into the heavenly kingdom. One can say without fear of error that the liturgical life fully realised is deeply submerged in a universe of figures and symbols which at one and the same time remind us that we are in exile and tell us of the mystery which makes us citizens of the City of God. And so we are invited to be attentive to the patterning of signs speaking to us from beyond our world and the clearest and most important of these, the sign which tells we have crossed the threshold of the eternal kingdom, is that of joy.

The coming of joy

What really is it, the liturgy? That is the question that Charlemagne asked one day of Alcuin his adviser and confidant. Alcuin's answer was that the liturgy is the joy of God. We could go further and say that it is the joy of God together with the joy of the whole creation.

One is reminded of the words of the *Exsultet* on Easter night: "Let the angelic choirs of heaven now rejoice.... Let the earth also rejoice, illumined with such resplendent rays." And the Preface for the Mass of Pentecost evokes the joy of the created world at the descent of the Holy Ghost upon the Apostles: "Wherefore does the whole world rejoice with exceeding great joy!" In the same way the *Sanctus* describes a universe filled to overflowing by a tide of divine glory: "Heaven and earth are full of your glory." And other texts from Paschaltide: "In him the heavens and earth rise again to life. In your resurrection, O Christ, heaven and earth rejoice, Alleluia!"

This joy which is according to its degree, an echo or a foretaste of the joy of heaven, is expressed liturgically in lyrical terms, by chanting, lights, white vestments, processions.

The chant of the Church we call Gregorian is an echo of the chant arising in the Heavenly Jerusalem. At Mass and during the Office the chant is not an optional extra simply to embellish the act of worship. It is on the contrary an essential part of Catholic worship, because worship on earth is in imitation of that worship in heaven which is a chant of grace and of praise. In heaven it is the great panegyric of the Apocalypse where the choirs of the elect and of the angels stand about the Lamb of God singing Amen and Alleluia. *Amen:* and so all is well. *Alleluia:* and may God be praised. These, as St Augustine tells us, are the two cries of eternity. It was only in the twelfth century that the practice of saying low mass became at all common. Until then the "celebration of the divine mysteries" - and this was the way the Mass was described - was always accompanied by chant and incense because the oblation is at one and the same time a making present of the cross and a participation in the liturgy of paradise.

Gregorian chant expresses this reality better than all the other chants of earth because it takes us with it into an atemporal world which excludes all merely naturalistic modes of expression. Even during Holy Week the intensity of supplication and of grief does not interrupt the serenity of a chant which derives from a point beyond grief - the same is true of the splendid chant of the

Orthodox - but with a note of joy about it which belongs only to Gregorian music. The music of the Renaissance, to be sure, was lit up with the fire of a new and incontestable beauty. But it is not the proper chant of the Latin Church. Neither can the bride of Christ recognise herself in the sounds of a more modern and expressionistic music, sensuous, emotional, indeed sentimental. Negro spirituals breathe an air of sadness and melancholy, and we seem to hear in their syncopated rhythm the sound of chains that bound the black singers of Louisiana. But in this form of religious expression there is lacking the light of Easter, the joy of heaven, the glorious freedom of the sons of God taken over into the Kingdom of his love.[7]

White clothing and the use of light remind us, too, of the life of heaven. They are derived from the most ancient parts of the Mosaic cult, and probably from primitive elements of an even more primal kind, linked with a natural symbolism. In the time of the early Church they had an essential role in the baptismal liturgy during which the neophytes wore a white linen alb to symbolise the fact that they had put on Christ. They received a lighted candle that marked them out as children of light: "Yesterday you were darkness, now you are light in the Lord. Walk as sons of light." These two ritual acts, accompanied by two final injunctions, form the last part of our present baptismal rite. They have come down to us as witnesses to a theology of clothing and of light that gave expression to joy.

The processional element in the liturgy is always expressive of the march of redeemed humanity towards the sanctuary of heaven. The Church, of course, is itself the image of paradise. This can be seen in the architecture of our temples of stone: the great doors of our cathedrals adorned with sculpture representing the elect mark the point of separation from the profane world and the entrance into the heavenly world. All liturgical processions finish at the sanctuary and imitate the upward movement of human life towards eternity. And this is the meaning suggested by the prayers which accompany the Candlemas and Palm Sunday processions, and those found in the monastic customaries.

In the ceremony of the *Dedication of a Church* the dramatic character of the entrance into the sanctuary is further emphasised by the ritual action of the triple knocking on the closed door of the church. The bishop knocks three times with his crozier (which symbolises the cross) at the door of the church, behind which the deacon and his acolytes represent the angels, and there is a solemn exchange of words.

The bishop sings: *"Elavamini portae eternales...* be ye lifted up, O eternal gates: and the King of Glory shall enter in!"

Then the deacon: *"Quis est iste Rex gloriae?...* Who is the King of Glory?"

The bishop: *"Dominus fortis et potens, Dominus potens in praelio...* The Lord who is strong and mighty: the Lord mighty in battle."

Who could not see here, as one might see a watermark on paper, the whole eschatology of salvation? Jesus Christ, the great high priest, victorious by the wood of the Cross, enters into his heavenly temple to celebrate there at the end of time the eternal dedication. What is signified here is acted out by the participants in the liturgical drama.

In the Byzantine rite of Solemn Mass, the gifts are carried in procession from the sacristy to the altar. The clergy representing the whole angelic hierarchy chant the *cherubicon*: "We who in mystic terms represent the Cherubim and who in honour of the life-giving Trinity sing the thrice holy hymn, set aside all worldly care in order to receive the King of all things, invisibly accompanied by all his legions of angels. Alleluia!"

The heavenly sacrifice

Much has been written about the idea of the *heavenly sacrifice* of Christ. It has been greatly championed by some and what seemed extreme about the idea has been strongly criticised by others. Today agreement seems to have emerged, based not on the notion of an everlasting *sacrificial act* on the part of Christ the Priest in heaven (Holy Scripture, indeed, affirms on the contrary that Christ Jesus died once),[8] but upon the notion of a permanent *sacrificial state*: Christ, bearing the marks of his Passion, appears in glory as the glorious victim of a completed act of sacrifice.[9]

Provided one sets aside the theory of a sacrificial death reproducing itself in eternity, then the idea of the heavenly sacrifice remains a valuable one. Fr. de Condren, who has written a great deal on this subject, has some illuminating insights:

"This great sacrifice offered by Jesus Christ with His saints to God in heaven, offering Himself together with them, is the very same sacrifice offered on earth through the saints by the priests and the whole Church in the Holy Mass. But there is this difference, that the communion which the saints have with Christ in heaven is uninterrupted and eternal, whereas ours is only daily and temporary. Here on earth we are subject to the changes of the temporal order and to the necessities of our present life, but in heaven there is no span of time other than eternity and no occupation other than that eternal sacrifice and communion. In heaven the saints commune with God and with Jesus Christ in the fullness of joy because they see God face to face, they see Him as He is. Here we commune with God without seeing Him, and we see him only with the eyes of faith... In the old law there were only prefigurings without the truth itself. Now we possess the Truth underlying those prefigurings. In heaven, in that place of joy and light, we shall have the same truth but uncovered and unveiled." (Condren)

How are we then to express the relation that exists between the Mass, the cross and the glorified Christ? One will say naturally, in the words of the Council of Trent, that the Mass is the sacramental renewing, in an unbloody fashion, of the sacrifice of Calvary. But we must see, too, that the Council of Trent affirmed this against the Protestants who denied that the Mass was a true sacrifice and sacramental offering of a true victim. The Tridentine definition did not intend to overshadow that other aspect of the sacrifice which the Fathers of the Church explained so well: namely that the Mass is in direct relationship with the liturgy which takes place in heaven. There is indeed an absolute identity between the Host placed on the corporal and the Heavenly Lamb, the Lord (*Kurios*) in glory.

One can say without fear of error that the Mass *is* in fact the heavenly sacrifice, because what the priest celebrating Mass for us holds in his fingers *is* in reality the glorified Christ, offering himself at that moment to his Father in majesty. This is why there is no special sign at Mass to represent the heavenly state. *The eucharistic bread itself is a heavenly reality: "panem coelestem accipiam...".* This is what is admirably suggested by the prayer *Supplices te rogamus*[10] (after the consecration). The commentators writing about this prayer in the Canon all speak in a realistic way, not of Christ descending from heaven by a kind of bilocation to be present suddenly between the fingers of the priest - this would be a metaphysical absurdity - but on the contrary, of the earthly community coming to have access to a higher plane of being so as to take hold of their risen Saviour as he is in his glory.

Florentius the Deacon emphasises the texts where St Augustine celebrates the invisible altar upon which the divine High Priest offers the eternal sacrifice of praise, for "the whole society of the redeemed, that is the whole great assembly of the saints, offered to God in a universal sacrifice by the one great Priest in paradise."

40

The prayer *Supplices* and the patristic commentaries upon it free us from a false theology of sacrifice whose tendency is to give the impression that Our Lord, enclosed as it were in the host is there somehow diminished (*in statu decliviori*). We are thinking of such unfortunate expressions as "the divine prisoner of the tabernacle" and other flowers of eloquence more sentimental than strictly true that were particularly dear to nineteenth-century preachers. The perspective of the fathers of the church and of other writers nourished by the same ancient tradition is by contrast solemn and profound: "there is a sacrifice in paradise which is at the same time offered upon earth since the host at our Mass is that which is present upon the heavenly altar, with only this difference, that here It is concealed by veils and symbols while there It is unveiled, undisguised." (Olier).

The angels in our midst

In the light of the above kind of commentary we understand better the allusion to the presence of the angels in the Catholic rite. Already at the beginning of the Mass it is in the presence of the whole court of heaven and of St Michael the Archangel that the faithful confess and strike their breasts. The incensing of the altar is likewise by the intercession of the Archangel, "who stands at the right hand of the altar of incense" (Roman Missal). During the *Gloria* the earthly community associates itself with the liturgy of the angels praying in *one voice* with them (*una voce* - the phrase is profoundly significant and deserves thought) to chant together the *trisagion* the angelic hymn which excels all others, the supreme chant whereby the Seraphim adore the thrice-holy God who lives in *inaccessible light*. According to St John Chrysostom in the chanting of the *trisagion,* "man is as it were himself transported to the heavens above, he takes a place close to the throne of glory; he takes wing with the Seraphim, he sings the sacred hymn."

There is no shadow of hyperbole in that great Doctor of the Church's words. The Mass is a mystic adventure of incalculable import. The mystery of the bloody cross is as it were re-presented with a tearing of the seamless robe of paradise. Jacob's dream becomes reality: the angels ascend and descend and their sympathetic presence makes sweeter our own participation in the austere sacrifice. When we approach our earthly altars we set in motion a friendly and admiring response on the part of our invisible brothers in heaven. In his *Tractatus Mysteriorum* St Ambrose speaks of the light that then comes upon us: "You make to approach the altar; the angels have their eyes upon you and they see this; and they see that whereas before you were a wretched sight, now suddenly you are radiant with light."

But it is our communion in the eucharistic sacrifice, which will actually make real what the psalms, the lights and the symbols all signify. Sacramental communion does not only allow us to "receive" the body, blood, soul and divinity of Our Lord; it also unites us in a kind of symbiosis with the cultic action of the beloved Son as it unfolds in the heavenly sanctuary. We are at one with Christ in His action as priest and victim. The knowledge of this leads to a *co-operation* on our part in an order of reality in which the boundaries between heaven and earth fade away. In the twelfth chapter of his epistle to the Romans St Paul exhorts the faithful to offer their bodies as "a living sacrifice, holy, pleasing unto God (*sicut hostiam viventem, sanctam, Deo Placentem*)."

The apostle's counsel finds its most perfect fulfilment in the very act of sacramental communion which makes the communicant a player in a liturgy at once angelic, filial and celestial under the loving gaze of God his Father and Creator.

We come now to the third part of our meditation on the liturgy. Let us consider the intimate relation which exists between man and rite, the way the rite can educate the man, and the danger involved in any slackening of this vital link. The Christian soul is so used to the sacred character with which, in the midst of the sanctuary, even the least liturgical action is imbued, that there is a risk that, so habituated, it will no longer fully take in the startling message addressed to it and will not really notice the void that will follow upon its disappearance.

Man and Rite

IN every country in the world, before learning to read and write, little children play, sing, conjure up great mysteries, clap their hands and chant nursery rhymes with an almost liturgical precision of rule. They do this without knowing they are making eternal and not only temporal sense. Down the ages man has felt the need to contain his joy and freedom within a perfect figure which is the image of eternity. Attracted by the circle as by a magnet, the men of antiquity saw in this shape the great law of the universe. They saw there the constant cyclic return of the seasons and of the stars which human life was subject to as to a majestic harmony from which it could not escape: *fatum*, the sacred expression of an overriding destiny.[11] The Hindus, led astray no doubt by a false metaphysic, but nevertheless ingenious constructors of parables, themselves have had recourse to the figure of the circle to express their vision of the world: this is the *round of Maya*, the twisting dance of illusion that carries away everything with it in a perpetual imprisonment of becoming, and from which the wise man must labour to escape.

The theme of the circle is found in a Christian perspective in Romanesque architecture, alive with symbolic force and this time inspired by a powerful realism, since it is no longer a case of expounding by means of the circle the endless round of illusory appearances, but rather of unfolding in parable form the reality of the Kingdom of God. Under the unmoving vault which represents the heavens, the altar is placed at the centre of a semicircle which reaches out into the side chapels radiating from it. The sacred ministers, *circumstantes ante thronum,* (standing before the throne) are a sign of the great public act of praise of the Church Triumphant in the heavenly Jerusalem, of which our liturgy here below is a humble yet precious reflection. Standing about the altar, in a prescribed order which symbolises the hierarchies of heaven, the ministers, clad in their wedding garments, their white albs, give expression to a holy and tranquil certainty of belonging to another world, and to their faith in the certainty of the promises of God.

The patrimony of mankind

Because the holy rites of the Church are charged with a very precise significance, any change in the rites can set off a war, a schism or a heresy.

The liturgical rite is thought in action. It is human thought incarnated in gesture, capable of the most intense expressive force and of the most exquisite philosophical delicacy

The ripe fruits of a whole civilisation, hanging heavy in beauty, are often caught up in the civilisation's fall. Sometimes they survive it like a refined and fragile flower (think perhaps, for example, of the persisting and outdated etiquette of the French court). We forget that these sacred rites were first of all the poetry of mankind in his infancy, barbarous and crude but the expression of men who danced out their theology before they ever thought to write it down. These religious rites in their earliest manifestation form the very first graspable expression, from across the long night of the ages, to have come down to us from our remote ancestors. For well before we have any written inscription, any wall painting, any hieroglyph from primitive man, we discover in what survives of his funeral rites the first and moving witness to a belief in a reality beyond him. The dead man, his legs drawn up to his chest in a foetal position, is once more entrusted to mother earth like the seed of eternity.

Like a poem in action and as a vitally important instrument of religious expression, ritual action seizes hold of human existence in its entirety and directs it back towards its source. And it is not only rites of death which are a turning back to the source, but also the rites of prayer and sacrifice, those connected with eating and hospitality, the rites of birth and of marriage, the cults directed towards the gods of the city, towards one's parents and one's country.

In his book called *L'homme et l'invisible* (Man and the Unseen), the ethnologist Jean Servier writes: "Properly speaking we ought to call no man a savage. We should realise that men are equally endowed with intellect and with the capacity to think. These primitive men, indeed, seem to have a greater care of the unseen good than of the goods of this world, and to have little regard for the forces that limit and determine earthly life, whether geographical, economic, social or historical." And again, Servier notes: "All the evidence of man's activity in the world bears about it the mark of the unseen. Tombs are more numerous than houses, and temples more solidly built than dwellings." And he concludes: "The unseen accounts for man as he is found in traditional cultures as the air accounts for the bird. Death seems to him as familiar a thing as the setting of the sun and as necessary a part of the cycle of his redemption as birth. The initiation that he undergoes prints upon his flesh the seal of the unseen homeland with ritual actions that are in essence the same wherever they are found in space and time, and with a symbolic meaning always the same."

Throughout the course of history these ritual acts preserve unchanged their dual character, religious and social: whatever was to do with the social community was sacred. To work or to die for one's city was a religious act.

To understand properly that notion of liturgy that seems so familiar to us, we must be aware that its roots tap deep into the ground at the most ancient levels of civilisation. In times past when a citizen of an ancient Greek city formally undertook to equip a ship of war, or when he composed a chorus in honour of the gods - as in the *Persians* where Aeschylus celebrates the victory of Salamis - this sort of public act in the service of the state was called *leitourgia* (from *laos*, the people and *ergon*, work): whence our modern word "liturgy". Taken in its original sense, the word liturgy thus signifies at once responsibility, sacred function and public ministry, and one can easily understand how in consequence the liturgical act was essentially a social act.

We find ourselves here on the edge of a definition of liturgy. It is, as Dom Guéranger tells us, "the totality of symbols, chants and actions by means of which the Church expresses and manifests her religion towards God." And the Abbot of Solesmes emphasise the point: "[It] is therefore not simply prayer, but rather prayer considered in social terms." [12]

Pope Pius XII, in his encyclical *Mediator Dei*, adds a note of precision which illuminates the royal and sacerdotal role of Christ in every liturgical act: "The holy Liturgy is the public cult which our Redeemer renders as head of the Church to the Father...it is the integral act of worship of the whole Mystical Body of Christ, that is both head and members."

One could put the two definitions together and express the whole matter in a compact form of words which gives prominence to the nuptial union between Christ and his Church, by saying that the liturgy is the *chant of the Bridegroom and of the Bride.*

An unfathomable mystery

And see how our understanding of liturgy at a single move is immeasurably enriched. It is no longer a case simply of the religious act of a community, expressing the sacrificial will of a people or of a city; it has become that unfathomable mystery on which the angels desire to look:[13] the marriage union between Christ and his Church, the act of the Word of God taking hold of humanity and raising it far above itself by virtue of his sacrifice. We have to do now with the whole great drama of redemption which has as its end the bringing together of all things whether in the heavens above or on the earth beneath and the subduing of them to the kingship and the priesthood of the well-beloved Son, "unto the praise of His glory." [14] This is the reality which liturgy enacts for us. It brings together within its compass the whole mystery of Christ; it conveys to us in an unbloody manner and under the gentler appearances of bread and wine, the bloody and triumphal drama of Christ, Priest and King. That is why this liturgical action is surrounded with so much solemnity; that is why a simple low Mass, not for the whole community and not sung, would have seemed rather strange to the first Christians. This is because their communities were so alive with the feeling of participating in a mystery which victoriously consummates the history of salvation, viewed as the wedding feast of the Lamb of God.

For those first Christians this solemn action was so profound, so ineffable in its significance that they could find no word adequate to denote the liturgical action. They used instead the single word *mysteria*, in the neuter plural (the mysteries) to describe it, or alternatively *sacramenta*, which signifies exactly the same thing or again *sacro sancta*. The Mass and the sacramental world that derive from that central act constituted the highest expression of the Christian life.

It seems that the feeling these first Christians had of participating in this union of heaven and earth,[15] and in the divine cult of the heavenly Jerusalem - whose splendour was the theme of the prophets of old - it seems that this feeling was decisive in stirring their souls to the generosity of martyrdom, giving them as it did the benign vision of eternity, an eternity which the reality of persecution and death constantly confronted them with.

To the end of time the Christian soul will find in the liturgy of the church the same source of life that quenched our fathers' thirst and the same heavenly vision that nourished their hopes. Perhaps even in our days, as in the time of the primitive Church, the liturgy could still teach a materialist world to look beyond its own leaden skies and to rediscover the savour of eternity.

The benign influence of the liturgy

It is often said that modern man is agonised and insecure. If he has lost the integrity of his inner life it is because his intelligence, turned in on itself, does not properly engage with external reality. Similarly his affections are adrift from the natural affections of the human heart; and his body, separated from whatever touches upon the life of the soul and having lost the secret of its own high calling, feels itself estranged from any kind of participation in the religious life. It should not surprise us then that this body should look eagerly to the pleasures of the senses and then find them nothing but a source of suffering.

At the opposite end of the scale, by contrast, St Paul writes to the faithful in Rome: "I beseech you, therefore, brethren, by the mercy of God, that you present your bodies as a living sacrifice, holy, pleasing unto God, your reasonable service."

Holy Mother Church has given us in the liturgy

a school of spiritual growth, in which we may learn the primacy of contemplation, in which we may feel the reality of the Church, where we may come to know beauty, come to love the regular ordered life and come to feel the sweet attraction of heaven.

The primacy of contemplation

It is principally thanks to its contemplative value that the liturgical tradition, faithful to the theology of St John, St Paul and the Fathers of the Church, offers a permanent remedy against the forces of disintegration which have menaced Christendom since the Renaissance.

The real evil of the Renaissance was not, as sometimes people affect to believe in order the better to excuse it, the return to the paganism of antiquity. It was rather the ferment of naturalism implied by this pseudo-restoration. For there is a great difference between the religious universe of the Greco-Roman world where piety and whole sections of religion remained intact and where the gods manifested themselves in the midst of the human world with ease and candour , and the religious world centred on man that the Renaissance brought with it. The misdeeds of a naturalism injected into the veins of a revealed religion presented dangers of a different order from the blind gropings of the pre-Christian religions. Liturgical prayer offers one great remedy against the temptation of naturalism: it insists on the prime importance of contemplation. The turning towards the light, the filial and loving contemplation of God, these things faithfully follow the delicately marked traces of a very ancient spirituality. Faced with a naturalistic energy turned in upon itself, the liturgical order opposes to it a long and continuing protestation of the holiness, the beauty and the grandeur of God. The pygmy man technocrat stands in wonder before the manufactures of his technological civilisation; he gazes upon the works of his brain, he looks down admiringly at the tools in his hands, and then looks further in still at the wonder of himself. But Holy Church straightens him up and sets him to prayer; her liturgy works upon him to make him little by little to forget himself, lose interest in himself, in his own hands, even to forget the blemishes and stains of his own heart. He gazes now upon the glory of another and sings in praise: *"Laudamus Te, benedicimus Te, adoramus Te, glorificamus Te, gratias agimus Tibi propter magnum gloriam Tuam!"*[16]

The Church herself is here in the first instance the contemplator of the glory of God, and she mediates for man the brightness of a light that would wound his eyes. She speaks to him of the secrets of her most high destiny, which is to become one with God. She leaves him dazzled by the sublimity of her calling, and places on his lips that inarticulate faltering of the prophet Jeremias,[17] an *alleuia* without words which brings one to see that the chant of the liturgy is simply an exalting, an ecstatic response to the promises of God that cannot be reduced to words: "This is why," says St Augustine, "he who exults does not use words but simply makes a joyous sound without words." This is the voice of the spirit lost in joy, expressing joy with all the strength at its command, but never coming to the point of reducing it to definition... And to whom is such exultation more fittingly addressed than to Almighty God in his ineffable glory? Ineffable is what cannot be spoken in words; but if you cannot and must not remain silent, then what remains but to exalt without words, your heart filled with wordless joy, whose immensity knows no limitation of syllables and letters?"[18].

At the heart, as we are, of a culture utterly absorbed in what is useful and saleable, we cannot insist too much on the educative effect of the divine liturgy. Absorbed for its part by the vision of eternity, and with all its concern being to bring men to an appreciation of what is gratuitous and disinterested, to fill their heart with song and exultation, it is the liturgy of the Church which will bring them to the place where all words fail, so that there they may love, praise and adore in silence "the beauty which is beyond speech."

The sense of the Church

The instability of modern man derives in large part from the fact that he has lost his sense of community. The unstable individual, utterly turned in upon himself, needs to belong to some community, visible or invisible, if he is to continue to exist. What we have in mind here, of course, is not that kind of collectivist civil society whose effect is precisely to isolate individuals in a colourless and shapeless mass of humanity (and how can we not now at times see a rather similar state of things within the Church?). Rather let us turn to the Church, properly considered. The Church, the Bride and the Mystical Body of Christ is the most diversified, most highly structured and most extensively stratified society that exists. From top to bottom everything in the Church bears the marks of a sacred hierarchy which stems from its living centre. The Church triumphant with its celestial hierarchy of angels and the elect is our true home; the early mediaeval painters depicted the whole hierarchy of creatures ranged in order round the Lamb, their eyes wide open, hands joined in prayer, from the great Seraphim down to the souls in Purgatory preparing to ascend and take their place amid the numberless choirs. As all this takes shape in our hearts, then we begin to learn about eternity.

There is no handbook, no textbook explanation which can open our eyes to the *Mysterium Ecclesiae*; only the living parable of the liturgy with its ordered ceremonial can give us a sense of the mystery.

Some years ago Abbot du Bec Helluin described[19] how at the end of one High Mass at which various Protestant ministers had been present, one of them exclaimed simply, "I have seen the Church!". We can see ample reason for an exclamation of this sort in our celebration of the Divine Office, flowing out as it does from the altar, by the mediation of the deacon, in a river of light, chant, incense and sacred action, to envelop the community of the faithful - themselves true actors in the liturgical drama - in the nave of the church, where the sound of the liturgy meets and marries with the silence of the soul.

Not infrequently the majestically patterned ordering of psalms and prophecies that makes up the public prayer of the Church will lead a straying soul to the sanctuary, where the chanting of prayer will uncover for that soul the mystery of the Bride of Christ. A Jewish rabbi in the twelfth century is said to have been converted to the Catholic faith, seeing that the lyricism of the synagogue was surpassed by that of the Liturgy of the Church, and finding that the same Liturgy led him without difficulty to the true fount of Revelation. Dom Herwegen, abbot of Maria Laach, has explained why this should be: "It is in the Liturgy, chiefly in the missal and the breviary, that Holy Scripture shines forth in the fullness of its light and speaks with all its true eloquence. The Liturgy, in fact, is the lyrical voice derived from the intimate union between the two supernatural realities of Holy Scripture and Holy Church."

In the Roman poet Vergil we find strangely prophetic passages which cast light on the hidden depths of history. Vergil's hero Aeneas is met by a mysterious maiden who consoles him. He only realises that she is a goddess by the way she walks as she leaves him: *"Et vera incessu patuit dea"*[20] What the church has about her of the supernatural is similarly to be apprehended by her way of prayer, a thing of air and sky and heaven, which reveals her true nature even as it veils it.

The feeling for beauty

This thought leads us to emphasise another of the good things given us, coming down to us from Christian antiquity: this is the feeling for beauty, inseparable in our view from the concern for doctrinal truth. We may use a photographic image to say that it is beauty that fixes truth. The truth of doctrine is more often betrayed by gradual insipidity of taste than by spiritual error pure and simple. The feeling for beauty is one of the consequences of our human condition, endowed as it is with a sensibility that anchors it in the very midst of the visible world. Plato said that the beautiful is the splendour of the true; and in return, appropriately, beauty becomes the defender of that order of truth from which it springs. This is why our fathers loved beauty.[21] It is no matter of astonishment then that the inspired writers of the Old and New Testaments clothed their thoughts with words of such beauty, and first among these is Our Lord Himself. We might say the same of the Fathers of the Church and of the mystical writers. The words of the liturgy also obey the great law of beauty because it is the very law of creation, which is itself the language of God, the open book of his mysteries, his garment of light: *Deus amictus lumine sicut vestimento.*[22]

Any man seeing about him what is graceful may see too that it bears upon it the signature of what is divine. Thus the philosopher Henri Bergson writes: "A man who contemplates the world about him with the eyes of an artist will see grace shining through beauty and goodness shining through grace. Every created thing in the living movement registered by its particular form testifies to the boundless generosity of the life-giving principle. And it is not any awkward accident that leads us to use the same word grace both for gracefulness of movement and for that act of liberality which characterises the goodness of God." [23]

In the book of Ecclesiasticus we find a passage praising those who presided over the destinies of the chosen people: "Let us now praise men of renown, and our fathers in their generation... Such as by their skill sought out musical tunes and published canticles of the scriptures. Men rich in virtue studying beautifulness: living at peace in their houses - *pulchritudinis studium habentes, pacificantes in domibus suis*".[24]

In the above text, taken from the first Nocturn at Matins in the Benedictine office for the 13th November, the feast of all the Benedictine saints, the disciples of St Benedict acknowledge their own forefathers. They understand that the beauty of the prayers of the Church obliges them to live with a certain style and dignity.

We know of a young novice who confided to his father prior that without the splendours of the divine office to which he had been introduced during his novitiate he would not have persevered. The gentle orderly influence of the liturgy as day succeeds day creates a kind of atmosphere in which what can only be called a certain spiritual and bodily deportment, a smiling seriousness, a sense of the contribution of even the smallest actions to the harmony of the whole, a certain way of dress, of speech, a certain way of bending the head, all contribute to make the whole of man's life *one continual liturgical act of prayer in the presence of God*. Paul Claudel, Benedictine oblate as he was, has described this all-pervading atmosphere very well: "How splendid a thing it would be if men in general worked with each other at their common tasks in real awareness of what they were doing, under the all-seeing eye of heaven, with an awareness of mutual help, of the ceremoniousness of co-operation with each other, of the praise offered to God by a simple raising of the eyes to heaven, of the delight of interchange with each other. There is something of all this in the Benedictine life. The life of the monk is not only chanting in choir, the returning of thanks and praise for each portion of time that is allotted to him by his creator; there is also the ordinary round of daily life, awaking, the garden, work, the meal eaten in common together with almost the solemnity of the Mass itself. There are these clothes one is washing, this lamp one lights; and these are profound symbols; the sick man one cares for; this visitor who rings the bell. If men in general only attended with greater awareness to the significance of what they were doing together as they were doing it, then they would themselves begin almost to think themselves in church, in choir. How much love there really is between men, without their being aware of it; and how splendid it would be if they were aware of it! The things men do without realising what they are doing they should rather do with conscious attentiveness. And then there would be nothing profane left in the world. All would be holy, consecrated to God." [25]

The love of rule and order

Liturgical spirituality would not be complete if one did not find the Cross there as well. Certainly it can happen that one finds oneself singing the alleluia of Easter morning with a heavy heart, for the Cross can make its presence felt within us at any time. The liturgy, however, proceeds inexorably, and it is this very inflexibility of its rule that saves those who take part in the prayer of the liturgy from their own particularity, their own imaginings, from dwelling upon their own state. [26] The sacrificial obedience of the man at prayer towards the rule of prayer can at first seem a heavy burden; but this submission of oneself is homage rendered to the transcendence of God.

It is truly said that all great art demands an ascetic discipline which at the outset, as it were, will save it from itself, from self indulgence.[27] All the more is this true of *ars orandi* which is the queen of the arts; it will shun whatever smacks of improvisation or vulgarity. Baudelaire was right when he said that "whatever is beautiful and noble derives from reason and conscious devising."[28] Today we live in a time of unbridled romanticism where a frenetic instability, libertarianism, a devotion to notions of evolution and progress all tumble together in confusion. Against these things stands the wisdom of all the ages.

"It does not surprise me," writes the French philosopher Alain, "that the Church dreads change of even the slightest sort. Long experience has shown her that true peace of soul presupposes unhesitating prayer on the lips, and this in turn means that things are always said in the same way." And he adds this: "Those who say over and over to themselves a familiar text until the meaning breaks forth from it are the true thinkers." This is exactly what monks have done for many hundreds of years in reciting the psalms. Today they are for changing all that, but the writer Thibon has wise words of warning for them: "Put no faith in the breakers of rules who claim to speak in the name of love. Wherever the rule is broken love too comes to nothing."

Subjection to some law is not only essential for the faithful carrying out any human work. It is not only what protects every human enterprise against a universal natural tendancy against disintergration; it is also itself an image of the eternal reality. This is why the divine work of the creation is characterised above all by order and stability. Paul Claudel, who in the forms of his poetry is among the most anarchic and unpredictable of poets, speaks of this in a passage which deserves to be quoted because it expresses the idea so well:

"Nature as each new season begins is not like some fashionable clothes designer racking his brain for new styles. We see her, on the contrary, never tiring of producing the same leaf, the same rose, the same bird, the same butterfly (always the old things).... She feels that so great an interest, so great an importance attaches to each of the things she makes that she never ceases to repeat each one like a child saying over and over again a word that he has not managed to make us understand... We also see a similar phenomenon where religion is concerned. Men of small and superficial spirirtual understanding, heretics, and modernists, are forever itching to get their hands on things, to change everything to radically reorder everything. The church for her part remains attached to the unchanging order of her doctrine and her ceremonies seeing, in the words of genesis, that these things are not only good but very good. In her psalms and hymns, in every morning's Mass, in the great poem of the liturgy at once both a dramatic action and a chorus, which stretches out through the whole year, the souls of the faithful, thirsting for love and for beauty, constantly find the living satisfaction of their desire, as also their fathers did before them."

The sweet attraction of heavenly things

We must count it one of the blessings conferred upon us by a schooling in the ancient discipline of the liturgy, that it not only persuades us to fall out of love with our own passions, but that it gives us the sweet taste for heavenly things, a thirst for God and for eternal life more precious than any other earthly reality. For there are two ways of fighting against that tumult of created things which fills the human heart: we may do it by our own human efforts, or, by the help of God, in contemplating supernatural things. These two ways, both of them good and necessary, occupy very different parts of the field of spiritual effort and give it very distinctly different colourings. The second of the two ways we call the anagogical or theological way, a way which puts impurity to flight by the force of love, by the attraction of light, by the savour of heavenly things. This corresponds to the first ages of Christianity, to the spirit of the liturgy and of the Fathers of the Church. It takes for granted the ascetic but goes beyond it.

The first way, owing more as it does to the natural operation of the powers of the soul, corresponds to those ages deeply influenced by the humanism of the Renaissance. It can hardly be a matter for surprise that the spiritual life should be in some way tributary to the tendencies and informing spirit of a given civilisation. From the sixteenth century onwards a certain kind of naturalism makes its appearance in the recommended methods of prayer where a taste for discursive meditation and introspection dominates, together with a recourse to psychology. At this time there begin to appear great saints and doctors of the Church whose role is to evangelise the more psychological realms of the human soul, seeking there the trace of the presence of Almighty God. Such was not the intention of the Fathers. Doubtless the struggle against self-love, idleness and sensuality required that considerable effort be allotted to clear away clinging and choking brambles from the path. But what provided the impetus driving on to the goal, what attracted one to the light *was none other than the light itself*. Modern man asks himself how he is to struggle against the sin of impurity. Our masters in the old tradition of the spiritual life are at one in their answer: *by lifting up your eyes to heaven*; for it is only the hope of heaven that will give man the courage to labour for it.

The rule of St Benedict, a rule of Christian life since the sixth century, gives a very clear illustration of what I mean. The subject of chastity is touched lightly upon in two places, with great discretion, and this is all that is said: in chapter IV *castitatem amare* (to love chastity) and in chapter LXXII *caritatem fraternitatis caste impendant* (let the monks practise a fraternal charity with chaste love). Nothing further. On the other hand, St Benedict in his rule treats at length of the search for God, of the imitation of Christ, of prayer, of the chanting of psalms, of the ineffable sweetness of love and of the "perfect love which casts out fear" (Prologue to the Rule). The experience of fourteen centuries of monastic life inclines one to think that the best way of avoiding sin is found less in the direct effort of turning away from it than in keeping one's gaze fixed steadily on God. We do little honour to the divine

Light and to its power of attraction if we choose some lesser focus for our energies in the fight for sanctity.

Dom Romain, founder and first abbot of En Calcat, described the high ground of the monastic life as being not the bodily mortification which of course he practised, but "the service of God, the coming joyfully into his presence, by means of the ancient prayer of the Church." And his successor, Dom Germain, gave this advice to his young monks: "When you are tempted you must use the word of God and the chanting of psalms to charm and lull yourself away from temptation as with a child who cannot have what he wants."

It has been said that the eyes are the barbs of hell. Are they not also the barbs of paradise? One cannot struggle against the hypnotic beauty of the flesh other than by invoking the beauty of a yet more powerful vision and one that resonates yet more profoundly within us. Claudel cries out against the moralists: "What is the use of so many theories, of so much explaining when we know instantly in any case that the dirt within us is at odds with the jewel?" [29] The exclamation of a modern man here joins hands with the thought of the men of old. The first monks who christianised Europe at the beginning of our era knew of the heavy dragging of the flesh and the necessity of spiritual combat. Their legendary feats of mortification at first glance seem to be what the monastic vocation is all about, but this is fail to see things in their proper perspective; not because these untiring strugglers against the flesh were not in reality given to ascetic practice but because before all that and in the very first place what they lived for was heaven. What wholly absorbed them was not their own struggle against themselves, but the contemplation of God, a contemplation lived out in the company of their fellow monks and in the practice of liturgical prayer where the body had a place, exercised a function. They did not contemplate sin the better to combat it, given that sin is no proper object for contemplation, but they fought sin the better to engage in contemplation, and their contemplation of God made lighter the strict discipline that makes up all asceticism.

The contemplative life, schooled by the liturgy, achieves something that could never be done by ordinary reflexive thought. It chooses to make use of created things, and with an exquisite tact in the choice: bread and wine, water and oil, incense and wax, and a sacred chant at the same time sumptuous and full of humility, whose unparalleled beauty itself yields to the overlordship of silence. It makes use of the ancient formulae of prayer, chiselled to a perfection that overcomes us, as though by the delicate beating of innumerable wings: and all this *in pursuit of the love of things unseen*. By a chaste attraction the light raises up within us that which merits entrance to the heavenly kingdom, whose excellence was intuitively felt by Simone Weil, a great soul who had not crossed the threshold: "Those who think that there is real nourishment to be had here below, or that one day there will be, are deceivers. Heavenly nourishment, by contrast does not only make the good grow within us, but it destroys the evil, the thing that our own efforts can never achieve. The amount of evil within us can only be lessened if we fix our gaze on that which is pure, without blemish." [30]

Even without their being aware of it, something will always be lacking to souls deprived of this light. This was the view of Dom Delatte. "The Church," he wrote, "has received from her heavenly Bridegroom, whose life she mediates and whose mission she fulfils, the sacred mode of prayer, the secret of that supernatural activity which attaches souls to God. If the Christian shies away from this life giving current, then at once his faith loses something of its vigor and simplicity; charity cools, devotion becomes merely personal, narrow, petty, confined to the arena of artificial and private feelings, to devotional practices of little real import and to books of devotion of little standing or authority." [31]

If one were to be asked what is the most striking characteristic, of all those which a filial and attentive spirit will uncover in the prayer of the Church, then one would hesitate between the poetry of the chant, the energy and focus of the influence exercised by the sacraments, the richness and variety of the sacramentals, and the sovereign remedy of those mysteries which imprint upon our souls the resemblance of our redeemer. But it cannot be doubted that the character of *holiness* evident even in the least important rite, the briefest formula, expresses better than all else the divine origin of the institution that we call the sacred liturgy. Thanks to its mysterious complicity with the choirs of the heavenly kingdom to which it gives access beneath the veil of faith, we are enabled to unite our voices to those of our brothers whom we do not see, and beneath their gaze, in suffering and in joy, to serve out our apprenticeship to eternity.

EPILOGUE

Addresses to novices

The prayer of the day

O you know to what wealth you are the heirs? At the end of the sixth century, at the moment when the Roman Empire, now utterly decadent, passed the torch of civilisation to the Christian world, the Church was already in possession of the greatest jewels of her liturgical treasure, among which we must count the *prayers of the missal* and especially the splendid *collects* which precede the reading of the Epistle.

Charles Péguy discovered with absolute delight that there is a saint for every day; you should know likewise that there is a prayer for every day to guide you along the narrow way.

You must know by heart these prayers, chiselled to perfection in the ages of faith, by delicate and skilled hands. You must study them and meditate on them because in the form of these sayings struck in bronze the purest spirit of Christianity is found. Nothing is more immediately apt for practical use than the great certitudes of the soul: our prayers are rules of life.

The name *collect* was given to the prayer which introduces the readings at Mass, and which we find at the end of each of the canonical hours, because it was recited in the presence of the faithful when they were assembled at the beginning of Mass. The *secret* and the *post-communion* verses owe their names to the places they occupy in the dramatic structure of the eucharistic sacrifice. The collect, like the preface, was at one time improvised at the will of the celebrant. Tradition has it that the *Te Deum* was recited for the first time by who pronounced the verses to each other alternately, in a kind of communal ecstasy. Then after this early period the Holy Ghost fixed the prayer of the young Church in permanent form, just as maturity fixes the characteristic traits of youth. There were whole collections of prayers, of which the most finely wrought have been preserved. One can recognise today the prayers for which St Leo the Great was responsible by their rythmic perfection and their rigour of thought; rule preserved inspiration by fixing excellence in permanent form.

To those nostalgically in love with the primitive Church and whose obsession is to see again a fluid creativity in the liturgy, we would reply that aside from it being incredible pretension on their part to wish such a thing, one cannot be a child more than once in a lifetime. Happily, thanks to the piety of our forebears who have handed on to us these jewels of our liturgy, a young barbarian coming to church to hear a Mass today is at once in direct contact with the thought, still fresh and alive, of one of the fathers of the fourth century.

Following a very ancient usage, the celebrant invites those present to communal recollection with the solemn admonition *Dominus Vobiscum* (the Lord be with you). The faithful reply: "And with thy spirit." The Lord must be with the priest so that he may be worthy to express the desires of the community. The Lord must be with the faithful so that they may be properly attentive to the prayer. The priest then prays aloud or chants the collect in a reciting tone in which just two notes marry with the literary form proper to the prayers of the missal. This is what is called the *cursus*. We will speak later of this literary device designed to underline the balance of the thought. Collections of prayers of this kind were made very early, certainly from the fourth century onwards, and they are part of the wealth of our liturgical inheritance.

You will find at the end of the Missal the collects one may add, according to need, to the prayer of the day. These are prayers for particular purposes: to ask for rain, to avert storms, to defend oneself against the devil, to beg for patience or chastity and an impressive prayer asking for that grace which is the gift of tears: *pro petitione lacrymarum*: "Almighty and most merciful God, who of old made a fountain of living water to spring forth from the rock of thy thirsty people, bring forth from the hardness of our hearts tears of compunction, that we may weep for our sins and by thy mercy obtain forgiveness for them."

Perhaps one day we will see academic theses on the rhetorical beauty of the prayers of the Church. The Breviary, Missal and Processional contain very many prayers remarkable for their elegance of form, their penetrating sweetness and their profundity of thought. Our collects are among the most ancient testimonies to the piety of the primitive Church; they have survived the slow transformations of the liturgy intact and they have great interest for us.

Two major characteristics should be emphasised: their doctrinal richness and the power they have to teach.

Richness of doctrine

The field of liturgy is itself a *locus theologicus* of inexhaustible wealth, a scattered network, as it were, of doctrinal truths with no systematic ordering. Péguy was right to describe the liturgy as a kind of "relaxed theology". Full of poetry, the chanting of the *Exsultet* arises in the night of the Easter Vigil, and the dogma of the Redemption illumines our understanding with its light, which is none other than the natural splendour of the truth. The *Exsultet*, the *Lauda Sion*, the *Dies Irae* are, as it were, chanted doctrine, infusing directly into the soul both light and love. Dom Guéranger once said, in words which were quite surprising at the time, that the liturgy was in fact Tradition in its most powerful and most solemn guise.

The matter of speculative theology is found in the Prayer of the Church just as the stones with which a church is built are found in the quarry. And theologians have always drawn upon this treasure in order to illustrate and affirm doctrine. Fr. Emmanuel, of Notre Dame de la Sainte Espérance, found the whole doctrine of grace in the prayers of the Missal. These prayers bear about them the marks of the doctrinal struggle against Pelagianism in the fourth century. Pelagius minimised the consequences of original sin and hence the necessity of *gratia sanans*, the grace that heals; and the heresy of Pelagianism is, of course, one of the ever-available forms under which naturalism re-emerges in each age. Fr. Emmanuel did not want to oppose thesis with thesis. Instead he built up his theology of grace on the foundation of the prayer of the church, and the prayers in the Missal helped him to bring into focus the absolute necessity of divine grace in the whole order of salvation. We have here a perfect illustration of the way in which the *lex orandi* prescribes and fixes the *lex credendi*. You will remember that recently a pentecostalist came to visit us. It was not difficult to demonstrate to him the disturbing novelty of a prayer addressed exclusively to the third person of the Trinity, simply by drawing attention to the trinitarian character of the collects in the missal, which turn to the Father by the Son in the Holy Ghost. Even the prayer for the feast of Pentecost keeps this form. The sequence at that Mass, an outpouring directed solely to the Holy Ghost, ought to be considered as a gloss on the Alleluia verse; the collect is still trinitarian. *"Nihil innovetur nisi quod traditum est."*

This, then, is what the liturgical collects teach us. And they teach us too the Majesty of God, the abyss of our own wretchedness, the way we should conduct ourselves before God, and the way to address Him if our prayers are to be granted.

The power to teach

The liturgy is also, and supremely, a model for prayer. Let us say that it offers us the most ancient and venerable of all the methods of prayer.

There has been much said about prayer and methods of prayer ever since the 16th century. St Teresa of Avila said that she felt like standing on the mountain top to convince all the world, if it were possible, of the importance of prayer. But from the 17th century onwards the practice of piety was greatly influenced by the humanism of the Renaissance, and prayer itself was subordinated to the desire of man to be himself investigating and doing. It was extremely unfortunate that the development of psychology inclined those given to prayer to devise *methods of prayer* which allowed a dominant role to analytical and discursive features.

Let it be said that for the first sixteen centuries of the Church's life prayer had never ceased to water the ground of the spiritual life. How then did the men of old pray? Did they use methods of prayer? It seems clear they did not. Prayer flowed out spontaneously from the heart of the Divine

Office. It was the river of the liturgical mysteries that refreshed the first Christian generations, like the four rivers of paradise; and these first Christians needed to devise no other way of access to the santuary of the inner life. In the ages of faith the liturgy was the great educator of the children of God. The hymns, the psalms, the chant, the whole sacramental order, poured into the souls of men the light of the truths of faith, and stirred men to look towards God rather than towards themselves, to celebrate the *mirabilia Dei* as they abdicated any sense of their own importance, just as the sculptors of old in carving the capitals in Chartres cathedral forgot themselves in the presence of their work. It was the influence of the liturgy that ensured a primacy for the contemplative life. The collects in the Missal then can to a remarkable degree show us what the liturgy has to teach.

You will notice first how important are the opening words of the prayer: a majestic invocation instantly brings us face to face with the omnipotence of God: *"Omnipotens sempiterne Deus..."* or alternatively it is the Church which is first mentioned: *"Ecclesiam tuam, Deus..."* or again, *"Familiam tuam..."* with here a note of gentle affection. Sometimes the prayer will begin with the abrupt vigour of a verb which throws into relief the hoped for action of God: *"Fac,*

Domine..." or "*Praesta, quaesumus Domine...*". Then after the opening phrase, the body of the prayer will express the petition being made, gracefully and economically put in very few words, so much so indeed that the central matter of importance about any feast day will be found perfectly encompassed in the words of its collect.

Here, as an example, is the collect of the midnight Mass at Christmas:
"O God, who has made this most holy night to shine forth with the brightness of the true light, grant we beseech Thee, that we who have known the mystery of his light on earth, may attain the enjoyment of his happiness in heaven."

With consummate art the liturgy takes us from a created reality to its uncreated analogue: from the light of Christmas night to the heavenly light, from the visible to the invisible. The collect of the Mass at dawn on Christmas day invites us to pass from being to doing: in a few words we are given the ground plan of Christian morality: that "the new light of Thy word made flesh may show forth in actions that which by faith shines in our minds - *in nostro resplendeat opere, quod per fidem fulget in mente.*"

And so each individual feast urges us to ask for its own particular grace, and with a delicate precision that leads the soul to the heart of the mystery being celebrated. We are brought to understand what is to be asked, how it is to be asked and why it is to be asked. The prayer for the feast of the Immaculate Conception develops harmoniously a fourfold shape [according to the four Aristotelian causes; formal, material, efficient and final]; that of the fourth Sunday after Easter entices us to raise up our hearts with a sweetness of language that only the Latin of the original will do justice to..."*ut inter mundanas varietates ibi nostra fixa sint corda ubi vera sunt gaudia* - that so, among the changing things of this world, our hearts may be set where true joys are to be found."

The Latin of these texts offer us prayers of such focussed beauty and precision that translation is often in reality impossible. How are we to translate words like "*hostia, pietas, devotio*"? At a distance of twenty centuries a modern vernacular word, even though often based on the Latin, seems somehow to have lost the substance of its meaning or to have suffered a semantic change.

Hostia means the victim of a bloody sacrifice and *devotio* signifies irreversible consecration. The word *pietas,* so washed out by current usage, would have need, in order not to be distorted, of a long paraphrase to give back to it its ancient, sacred vigour.

The *pietas romana,* that virtue central to the life of Rome, had at one and the same time a very earthly and a very spiritual meaning. It signified attachment to one's native earth, faithfulness, gratitude, also worship rendered to the gods, to one's parents, to one's native land, and devoted respect for family, for the domestic hearth, and for the shades of one's ancestors. One has some inkling, then, of just what this word could mean for the first Christians once they were baptised. The soul, enlightened by the Word, responded *sicut naturaliter* to the gentleness of the Father as it turned again to the blessing of its own home country in the life of the Triurne God.

Some of you will be asking yourselves how you can use the collects of the Missal for private prayer. The first thing is to *know how to read*, a knowledge not very widespread, contrary to what is believed, and which involves two operations: the scrutinising of what is said and the weighing of it. My advice to those of you who wish to nourish your own life of prayer with the public liturgical prayer of the Church is to do as you would if you were prospecting for gold. The cycle of the liturgical year is like a great river freighted with rituals, chants and poetry. One finds everywhere tiny phrases of two or three words shining brilliantly like specks of gold.

An excellent method of prayer is to read slowly the proper of the day from the missal and day after day to sift through, as it were, the water of this river and carefully to keep back whatever answers the soul's needs and desires.

The collect for the Sunday will become, with the Church leading us, both a richly various meditation and a very practical exhortation for the rest of the week. And so there will be graven upon our memories the formulae of our favorite prayers, our path lit up by such brightly shining fragments of wisdom as these:

Sic transeamus per bona temporalia,
ut non amittamus aeterna.[32]

Sacramentum vivendo teneant
quod fide perceperunt.[33]

Sine te nihil potest mortalis infirmitas.[34]

Ad promissiones tuas,
sine offensione curramus.[35]

Da nobis fidei, spei et caritatis augmentum.[36]

Discamus terrena despicere
et amare caelestia.[37]

Auctor ipse pietatis![38]

In the three words of the last fragment what power there is to deflect the heart towards almighty God: *Thou who art the author of all godliness.*

Could there be anything sweeter than to pray in the very words and language of those first Christians, newly reborn in the waters of baptism, hearing the things read that they heard, singing what they sang, listening as they did to the mysterious voice of the spirit, and of the bride saying: "Come, Lord Jesus!"

The whole of our existence is
a liturgical action

OU have asked me what kind of place is to be accorded to the liturgical life in our monasteries. I can reply without hesitation that it should be the chief place. The liturgy is for us a kind of daily resurrection. Thus when the monk on the morning of his profession, prostrate full length on the ground, hears the chanted cry of the deacon: *"Surge qui dormis et exsurge qui mortuis et illuminabit te Christus"*[39], he reaches out and touches that source of energy in the liturgy to which the first Christian generations adhered with all their being. The rest of us, too, as monks find here the whole of our spirituality; and this is why properly speaking there is no Benedictine spirituality. The monk is a man fashioned inwardly and outwardly by the liturgy. It is this fact which makes our own practice of religion so ample, so universal, so accessible to our contemporaries.

The idea that the sacred rites and words of the liturgy were in themselves nourishment enough for the soul, and a sure enough guide to the heights of mystical experience, without our needing to immerse ourselves in the spiritual treatise and theories elaborated in modern times, is one that lasted for sixteen centuries, during which time the fundamental character of western spirituality was shaped. To the degree that we remain faithful to this inspiration we join hands again with the first Christians. With them we look to the Heavenly Jerusalem; with them we play on that instrument which is the human body: hands, eyes, voice, the bending of the knee, the bowing of the head. Remember the words of St Augustine: "the affection of the heart is fostered by the gestures that render it." [40] Provided, of course, that those gestures retain their original purity and meaning. Christendom rose upon the human race like a dawn in the sky of history because the Christian soul, intent upon the religious rite, constantly saw the supernatural open out of the natural. The link between signifier and signified was a living one; every gesture actualised faith; nothing was lacking to the education of our fathers in the faith. All this gave human life a certain nobility. Charles Péguy understood this well; you may remember his memories of a childhood spent in the Bourgogne district of Orléans: "Everything was a rhythm and a rite and a ceremony..."[41]

In the ages of faith the Christian child grew up amid a multitude of human rites that spoke to him of the invisible world as clearly as the motorway sign points out to us the direction we are to take. And what is there to prevent us, too, a tiny group of monks in the great liturgical tradition, from absorbing into our being a sense of the real truth of symbols?

If we are asked what place the liturgy has in our monastic life, we answer with the voice of tradition that it is the whole existence of the monk, and even - why not? - that it makes up the whole of Christian life, which should be a liturgical reality. A monk's whole life will be nourished, illumined and governed by the rhythms of the sacred liturgy.

We have a very impoverished notion of baptism if we think of it only as a kind of "entrance ticket to heaven". We must go beyond this poverty stricken idea which is really derived from Protestantism. For the Protestants the sacrament is inefficacious in itself, no more than a legal title to the future life. Recall instead these decisive words from Holy Scripture: "But you are come to Mount Sion, and to the city of the living God, the heavenly Jerusalem, and to the company of many thousands of angels"[42] and again: "Now therefore you are no more strangers and foreigners; but you are fellow citizens with the saints and the domestics of God."[43] And this which is perhaps the finest of all the texts from the Epistles of St Paul: "But we all, beholding the glory of the Lord with open face, are transformed into the same image from glory to glory, as by the Spirit of the Lord."[44] It was from within a liturgical perspective that our own Father Abbot, Dom Romain, said to his monks one Christmas evening: "We are made for the holiest and most solemn things; we are made so that we may unceasingly move forward on the side of God."

This is so much as to say that consecrated souls cannot thenceforward behave other than in obedience to their new dignity. There is nothing stilted or artificial about this; something within them must inevitably express the nobility of their state; something within them must translate itself even into bodily gesture and carriage. You will remember the chapter for the ferial office at None: "You have been bought at a great price:

glorify God and bear Him about in your body - *Glorificate et portate Deum in corpore vestro.*" And is it not in great part thanks to the singular education of the monastic obedience that you begin little by little to change what you have habitually been? Is it not the case that the service of the altar and the discipline of choir very rapidly exert an influence upon your soul and your body? Instantly when the bell for Office is heard, see with what gravity you must pass down the nave, with what recollection you greet one another, turn towards the altar, and lose yourself in adoration at the *Gloria Patri.* And will all this cease when you cross the threshold of the chapel again to go to your work? Certainly not; rather the whole of your life will, as it were, be within the cloud of incense and will unfold in the presence of God and the angels. The whole of your life will have about it the holiness of offertory and consecration. And so the life of the monastery itself unfolds in one great liturgical procession, in which the soul pours itself out in secret, silent offering.

The humblest of tasks themselves also have imprinted upon them the marks of the liturgy since they begin and end with the sounding of the bell for choir. Our labours, alas, are not always as enthralling as all that! But performed in union with our Lord, who laboured at home in Nazareth, they can come to be a profound and mysterious liturgy. The words of Pascal seem very appropriate: "Do the little things as though they were great things, remembering that the majesty of Christ within us works them and lives our life; and do the great things as though they were no more than little things easily done remembering the power of Christ within us."

We see, then, why it is that the church is not the only place of worship within a monastery, but that rather the whole monastery including all the lowliest outbuildings is such a place. In times past it was always the refectory that most evidently resembled the church, with its formal vaulting, with the prayer chanted before and after meals, with the community assembled together in its proper hierarchy - this clearly visible in the seating arrangement - the reader at his lectern reading without a break, *recto tono,* some book to nourish the spirit as the body paused for refreshment. The monastic habit is also itself a school of prayer which disciplines the movements of the body. The professed monk, during the course of any ceremony, is always clothed in his cowl, in his choir robe. And as you know on his last day the monk is laid to rest in the earth enveloped in his cowl, to await the Resurrection of the dead.

The ritual surrounding the monastic cowl is composed of many layers of symbolic meaning. It is the image of the wedding garment which pre-figures for us that final clothing in heavenly glory; again it expresses the state of forgiveness and grace of the son reconciled with his father. (And how sweet and gentle a thing it is to know oneself at peace with one's Father!) The black cowl signifies a man bereaved of all the joys of the earth, and signifies also watching in the night, burial, the expectant waiting of a soldier or a servant.

The monastic cloister, a holy place to walk in, hushed in silence, leads nowhere. It is of a piece with the circular contemplation of which Denis the Areopagite speaks. And the final end of this never ceasing contemplation is an escape to the heaven above; upwards and not forwards, a spiritual and not an earthly overtaking, for our God lives in inaccessible light. There is not a single word, not even the most prosaic, which does not take on a sacral character, thanks to the parsimonious use we make of words and the ritual we observe on beginning to speak. The monk puts a finger before his lips and waits for a sign from his superior to indicate that he may speak. This sign, the word *benedicite,* aligns the words of ordinary speech with the words of benediction which we find in the canticles of the Divine Office. How strange a command this is: one may speak only to bless. Many times you ask me what is the secret of being able to live always in a state of prayer, always in the presence of God. The answer is a simple one: think of your whole life as a single great sanctified liturgical action; every part of it will then have its value because everything is done in union with Christ and in the sight of God the Father. In this way all our actions will be bound together in a deep unity. As St Paul says: "Whether you eat or whether you drink do all for the glory of God." The monk finds unity within himself and consequently not only within himself but within the rest of the created order.

For if the liturgy of the Church impregnates all our actions, it does not do so by isolating us behind walls that separate us from the rest of the world. Certainly we have chosen to close our eyes to the allurements of the world; but it is the miracle of the liturgy that it enables us to bring the created order together in a whole, in a great effort of transfiguration which is the work of sacred poetry. One cannot live without poetry. At any rate the Church has decided we shall not have to. She has placed upon our lips some of the finest poetry written to make of us the priests and poets of the Sacrifice of Praise. Bossuet in a famous passage locates man's priestly function at the heart of his calling, as a duty that cannot be abandoned. Man is to "give a voice, an intelligence, a heart on fire with love to the whole of the visible creation, so that in its turn, through him and by means of him, creation will love the invisible beauty of its Creator. This is why man is set in the middle of the world, a working synopsis of it..., a great world within the little world, because while by his body he is enclosed in his world, by his spirit and his heart he is greater than it; and contemplating the whole of the universe, drawing it into himself, he offers it, sanctifies it, and consecrates it to the Living God. Man is made the contemplator and the mysterious synopsis of all the variety of visible creation, so that through nature, by his holy love, he may be the priest and adorer of the invisible and intellectual creation."[45]

But this priestly function can only come to completion in Christ. For He alone can save, rule, take upon Himself, and lead that creation, which flowed from Him into space in the first days of Genesis, to its proper end. St Gregory of Nazianzen, in a sermon on the baptism of our Lord, describes Christ *"coming out of the water and in a certain way drawing the world after Him and raising it to Himself."*

And Peter the Venerable, abbot of Cluny, also witnesses to his sense of Christ the enlightener of the world in this splendid invocation:

> *Christe, Dei splendor,*
> *Qui splendida cuncta creati*
> *Kyrie Eleison!*[46]

You have in these great examples set before you, all that is necessary to enable you to accomplish by prayer this task of reuniting all things under the sceptre of Christ. The monk, whether or not he is a priest, should think of his vocation as a great spiritual adventure: every morning the new day that dawns opens for him a blank page, on which he will write the poem of his life. He can truly say with the psalmist: "My heart has uttered a good word: I speak my works to the king. My tongue is the pen of a scrivener that writeth swiftly."[47] His zeal in praising and in honouring God will indeed make of his whole life a single, uninterrupted chant, and this chant will lead him to advance in virtue, while his spiritual advance will in turn lead him to sing the glory of his Lord all the more. This reciprocity was the plan of life of the Benedictines of Cluny, and they found it perfectly expressed in one of the best known prayers of the missal: "*Gloriam Dei sempiternam et proficiendo celebrare et celebrando proficere.*" By spiritual advance the monk celebrates ever better the eternal glory of God, and by celebrating it he advances in sanctity.

O sacred liturgy, honour of the Church, you who have inspired so many works of art and poetry, who inspired St Francis, the little pauper, to sing the glory of his Lord on the roads of the world; you who put upon our lips the song of the elect, and govern our steps on the path to heaven; you who banish from our hearts all impurity and entice them towards the good that is invisible: we swear faithfulness to you until death and even beyond death, in that paradise of inexpressible splendour some part of which you open to us here.

BUT THE WORD OF GOD, THE SON OF DAVID, BEFORE EVER DAVID CAME TO BE, SET ASIDE THE LYRE AND THE CITHARA, INSTRUMENTS WITHOUT SOULS, TO BRING THE WHOLE WORLD, GATHERED TO-GETHER IN MAN, INTO HARMONY WITH HIMSELF BY HIS HOLY SPIRIT. HE USES MAN AS AN INSTRUMENT WITH MANY VOICES AND ACCOMPANYING HIS SONG WITH THIS INSTRUMENT WHICH IS MAN, HE PLAYS HIS MUSIC TO GOD.

Clement of Alexandria

NOTES

1. Romans viii.18-22.

2. "All things were made by him: and without him was made nothing that was made. In him was life and the life was the light of men." (John i.3-4)

3. "The tender body is pierced, blood and water flow out; with what a stream are earth, sea, stars and world washed clean!"

4. Psalms 103, 143, 76, cant. of Daniel 77, 97, 113.

5. *Les Parfums de Rome.*

6. St Angela of Foliguo.

7. Nothing expresses better the newly transformed condition of the Christian and the state of joy in which he finds himself than that striking phrase of St Paul: "Giving thanks to God the Father, who has made us worthy to be partakers of the lot of saints in light; who has delivered us from the powers of darkness and who *has translated us* into the kingdom of the Son of his love." (Col. i.12) The verb relates to an action that has already taken place: "*transtulit*: he has carried us across". Baptism has transported us into another world.

8. "Christ rising again from the dead dies now no more...For, in that He died to sin, He died once." (Romans vi.9-10). "Christ also died once for our sins." (1 Peter iii.18).

9. "I saw... in the midst of the throne...a Lamb standing as it were slain." (Apoc. v.6).

10. "We most humbly beseech You Almighty God, command these things to be carried up by the hands of thy holy angels to Your altar on high, in the sight of Your divine majesty..."

11. At Stonehenge, between Salisbury and Bristol, about 1500 years before Christ, men built a mysterious circle of stones which can be seen to this day. The circle was 90 feet in diameter - the 30 uprights weighing each about 25 tons supported a continuous circle of 30 horizontal slabs. Levy-Strauss, in *Tristes Tropiques*, observes with interest the circular structure of Bororo villages.

12. Dom Guéranger, *Institutions liturgiques*, chp.1.

13. 1 Peter i.12.

14. Ephesians i.14.

15. "A night in which heavenly things are united to those of earth, and things divine to those which are human!" (The *exsultet* from the Easter vigil).

16. It is striking that the sacred text first directs the action of thanksgiving of the faithful towards the good that is in God himself. It is thus that the liturgy trains the soul to forget itself, to lose sight of itself.

17. "And I said: Ah, ah, ah, Lord God, behold, I cannot speak, for I am a child!" (Jeremias i.6)

18. St Augustine, Enarr. super psal. 99.4, 32.1-8.

19. This was 30 years ago during the pontificate of Pius XII.

20. "And by her way of walking she was truly revealed a goddess." (Aeneid i.405).

21. We must rid ourselves of the illusion that truth can communicate itself fruitfully without that radiance

which is natural to it and which we call beauty; without our affirming, at least where writing and communicating our thoughts are concerned, that the souls to whom God has confided - by the means of his grace - the continuance of his own action in the temporal order have a new liberty with beauty. Beauty then is inseparable from truth. It is its splendour, it is the intellectual and sensible flower of that which is good. It is the radiance of being. For the Christian it cannot be merely a game, an entertainment. If it is separated out from the true and the good, it is as though the beam of light were separated out from the lighthouse that sent it out." (Henri Charlier, *L'art et la pensée*, p38 & 89.)

22. "God clothed with light as with a garment" (Psalm 103).

23. H. Bergson, *La pensée et la mouvant*.

24. Ecclus. xliv.1-6.

25. Paul Claudel, *conversations dans le Loir et Cher*, p 102.

26. It is the rule in the theatre to bring the play to conform to these essential conditions, and to elevate the action, even though it be profane to the edge of the sacred. Thierry Maulnier in his *Racine* entitles his sixth chapter: *La cérémonie tragique:* what he says here will also apply easily to the drama of the liturgy:
"Racine's heroes never stoop to the vulgar spontaneity of naturalistic gesture. They do not betray their emotions, they do not release them other than transformed into comprehensible signs, and by this passage through the process of thought they are defined, ordered, made intelligible... All the emotions expressed find in Racine's inflexible style a chaste exterior and at the same time a sublime inner intensity. These heroes, burning with frenzy, keep formal

distances between each other that are required not only by propriety but also by a dramatic rigour that will not allow the passions any physical release nor consequent loss of intensity... Distanced, dulled or veiled by everyday life, the deep forces of our fate within us deserve, when they appear in their burning energy, to be treated with respect. Classical Tragedy has a primitive and primordial quality about it that modern theatre has progressively lost. Because of the opportunity it gives to man to revere his own reality or to bewail his fate, because of its essential aim, its significance, its origins, the tragic theatre is essentially something very solemn."

27. Maritain, *Art et Scolastique*.

28. Baudelaire, *L'art dramatique*.

29. L'Oiseau noir dans le soleil levant.

30. Simone Weil *Réflexions sans ordre sur l'amour de Dieu*.

31. *Dom Guéranger,* by a monk of Solesmes.

32. "That... we may so pass through things temporal that we do not finally lose those which are eternal." (Collect for the third Sunday after Pentecost.)

33. "That they may retain in their lives the effect of the sacrament which they have received by faith." (Collect for Easter Tuesday.)

34. "Through the weakness of our mortal nature we can do nothing without You." (Collect for the first Sunday after Pentecost.)

35. "That we may run without hindrance towards the attainment of Your promises." (Collect for the 12th Sunday after Pentecost.)

36. "Grant us an increase in faith, hope and charity." (Collect for the 13th Sunday after Pentecost.)

37. "We may learn to despise earthly things and love those of heaven." (Post-communion for the feast of the Sacred Heart.)

38. "You who art the author of all godliness." (Collect for the 22nd Sunday after Pentecost.)

39. Arise, you who sleep, and come forth from the dead and Christ will enlighten you.

40. St Augustine, PL xl. col. 597.

41. "Everything was a rhythm and a rite and a ceremony... everything was an event, a sacred thing... Everything was an inward uplifting, a prayer; the whole day, sleep and waking, work, and what little rest there was, bed and table, house and garden, door and street, the courtyard, the doorstep and the plates on the table."

42. Hebrews xii.22.

43. Ephesians ii.19.

44. II Cor. iii.18.

45. Bossuet, *Sermon pour la fête de l'Annonciation*, 1662.

46. "Christ, the splendour of God, who has created all things in splendour, have mercy on us!" (ex epistola Petri Venerabilis IX LS VI Epist. xxxii).

47. Psalm 44.

DISCOVERING THE MASS

A Benedictine monk

IN THE MIDST OF THE LITURGICAL CRISIS WITH WHICH WE ARE ALL too familiar, this little book calmly lays forth the rich liturgical heritage of the traditional Roman Mass. What is a sacrament? What is the Mass? What is the liturgy? After addressing these questions, the author examines the detail, historical origin and meaning of the rites of the Holy Sacrifice of the Mass.

IT IS OUR PRAYER THAT THIS BOOK WILL IN SOME MEASURE HELP the faithful to appreciate and more profoundly to love the Mass, and so contribute to a deepening of what Pope St. Pius X called "that true Christian spirit" whose "indispensable fount ... is the active participation in the holy mysteries and in the public and solemn prayer of the Church."

WITH THIS INTENTION, WE RENEW THE CALL MADE BY DOM Prosper Guéranger over 150 years ago: "Open your hearts, children of the Catholic Church, and come and pray the prayer of your Mother!"

paperback, 120 pages, ISBN 1 901157 06 7, £9.95

FOUR BENEFITS OF THE LITURGY

A Benedictine monk

"The young people who come on retreat to the monastery often wonder why we give so much importance to the liturgy in our monastic lives. One of our novices, now a monk and a priest, who underwent harsh trials during his noviciate, supplies the answer. One day he confided: 'I would not have persevered in my vocation if God had not, by the grace of the holy liturgy, given me a helping hand each day during the course of the year.' ... In the very depths of our souls the liturgy works a sort of seductive charm."

THE LITURGY IS THE SOUL'S MYSTICAL SCHOOL, FORMED DURING the course of two millennia of Christian spirituality. In this collection of meditations, the author develops four themes relating to the liturgy:

- The primacy of adoration
- The splendour of the liturgy
- The sense of the Church
- The formation of the interior man

paperback, 36 pages, ISBN 1 901157 08 3, £1.95

The Saint Austin Press' Titles

GENERAL SACRAMENTAL ABSOLUTION
Scott M. P. Reid
In this scholarly account, Reid argues that the use of General Absolution is not an appropriate response to the decline in confessions. A wide-ranging historical, canonical and pastoral perspective.

40 pages, paperback - stapled, £1.95 ISBN 1-901157-65-2

LIFE OF ST. EDWARD THE CONFESSOR
St. Aelred of Rievaulx
Translated into English for the first time by Fr Jerome Bertram, FSA. St. Edward built Westminster Abbey and was a great friend of the poor. An inspiring account of the life and miracles of England's Saintly King.

138 pages, paperback, £9.95,ISBN 1-901157-75-X

THE SIMPLICITY OF THE WEST
Peter Milward, S.J.
This work charts the idea of simplicity - as seen in the context of nature and tradition - through Socrates, St. Francis, St. Thomas Aquinas, to the present day. An exhilarating tour of Christian civilization with a profound message.

95 pages, paperback, £9.95, ISBN 1-901157-95-4

A BITTER TRIAL
Evelyn Waugh and John Carmel Cardinal Heenan on the Liturgical Changes *(Ed. Scott M. P. Reid)*
For the last decade of his life, Waugh experienced the changes being made to the Church's liturgy as "a bitter trial." In Heenan he found a sympathetic pastor and kindred spirit. This volume contains the previously unpublished correspondence between these prominent Catholics, revealing in both an incisive disquiet.
71 pages, paperback, £3.95, ISBN 1-901157-05-9

The Saint Austin Press' Titles

THE EARLY PAPACY
to the Council of Chalcedon in 451
Adrian Fortescue
A clear exposition and sound defence of the belief in the role of the Pope in the Church, drawing upon evidence from the Church Fathers up to 451 AD.

96 pages, paperback, £7.95, ISBN 1-901157-60-1

THE FACE OF THE NAZARENE
Noel Trimming
This dramatic and involving story is also a profound meditation on the Lord of the Millennia; Jesus Christ, the same yesterday, today and forever. It charts the impact of Christ on some of the people who knew him, in the hectic circumstances of their everyday lives.
157 pages, paperback, £9.95, ISBN 1-901157-90-3

NEWMAN'S MARIOLOGY
Michael Perrott
A study of the development of Newman's beliefs about Our Lady, from the staid "Anglican red-letter days" of his time in Littlemore to the intimate and inspiring poetry of "The Dream of Gerontius" and his "Meditations and Devotions." Scholary but immensely readable.
104 pages, paperback, £8.95, ISBN 1-901157-45-8

THE CATHOLICISM OF SHAKSPEARE'S PLAYS
Peter Milward, S.J.
The local tradition in Stratford is that Shakespeare "died a Papist." Professor Peter Milward, of Sophia University, Tokyo, argues that the whole of Shakespeare's work reveals a common thread of sympathy with the plight of persecuted Catholics under Queen Elizabeth and King James I.
144 pages, paperback, £7.95, ISBN 1-901157-10-5

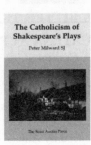

The Saint Austin Press' Titles

A VICTORIAN CONVERT QUINTET
Rev. Michael Clifton
In this fascinating study of the faith journeys of five converts to Catholicism from the Oxford Movement, Fr. Michael Clifton invites the reader to consider the lessons we might learn from this *Quintet* of learned men.
212 pages, paperback, £9.95, ISBN 1-901157-03-2

DARKNESS VISIBLE
A Christian Appraisal of Freemasonry
Rev. Walton Hannah

Addresses the question of whether involvement with Freemasonry is compatible with one's duty as a practising Christian. It includes the entire and authentic text of the Masonic ritual of the first three degrees and of the Royal Arch.
232 pages, paperback, £12.95, ISBN 1-901157-70-9

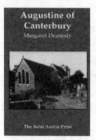

AUGUSTINE OF CANTERBURY
Margaret Deanesly
This study deals with St. Augustine's training, character and background; the origins of his mission; his work in Kent; the structure of the church he established; the nature of the ministry he founded for the continuance of his work.

175 pages, paperback, £12.95, ISBN 1-901157-25-3

CATENA AUREA
A Commentary on the Four Gospels
St. Thomas Aquinas

Drawing completely on the Church Fathers, St. Thomas provides an indispensable verse by verse commentary on the Gospels. Translated under Cardinal Newman, introduced by Aidan Nichols OP.
2,825 pages, hardback, 4-volume set, £85,
ISBN 1-901157-40-7

The Saint Austin Press' Titles

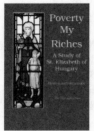

POVERTY MY RICHES
A Life of St. Elizabeth of Hungary
Sr Elizabeth Ruth Obbard ODC
An inspiring account of the thirteenth-century wife, mother and queen who endured suffering all her life and died among the poor and sick whom she loved so much. A woman's account of this life of extraordinary sanctity.
106 pages, paperback, £9.95, ISBN 1-901157-80-6

THE VENERATION AND ADMINISTRATION OF THE EUCHARIST
The Proceedings of the 1996 Second International Colloquium on the Liturgy, organised by the Centre International d'Études Liturgiques (CIEL).
Includes papers from leading theologians and explores aspects of the traditional Latin liturgy and the development of the Church's Eucharistic teaching.
255 pages, paperback, £12.95, ISBN 1-901157-15-6

ALTAR AND SACRIFICE
The Proceedings of the 1997 Third International Colloquium of historical, canonical and theological studies on the Roman Catholic Liturgy, organised by the Centre International d'Études Liturgiques (CIEL).
An inspirational and fascinating collection of academic papers on the traditional Roman Liturgy given by international experts.
192 pages, paperback, £12.95, ISBN 1-901157-85-7

THE CEREMONIES OF THE ROMAN RITE DESCRIBED
Adrian Fortescue & J.B.O'Connell
A reprint of the 1962 edition of this classic ceremonial manual for the traditional Latin Mass. Published to support the work of the new traditional religious communities in union with the Holy See.
424 pages, hardback, £24.95, ISBN 1-901157-00-8

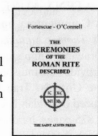

The Saint Austin Press' Titles

THE THREE YS MEN
Joseph Pearce

In his first novel, the author of the best-selling biography of Chesterton, *Wisdom and Innocence*, undertakes a journey through Sussex in the company of three myterious ghosts. These are Yore, the Ghost of Sussex Past (the thinly disguised ghost of Hilaire Belloc); Yo the Ghost of Sussex Present; and Yet, the Ghost of Sussex Future. En Route, the three spirits have many misadventures and can seldom agree on anything, constantly arguining about the relative merits of tradition and modernity in relation to time and eternity.There is also a suprise appearance of Tim, the Ghost of Time Uncompleted (the thinly disguised Ghost of HG Wells). The final chapter adds several twists to the tale. 176 pages, hardback, £13.95, ISBN 1-901157-02-4

THE INVISIBLE CROWN
Michael McGrade

Amongst the Glorious litany of Catholic saints, who has heard of Nicholas and Dorothy von Flüe? Yet this fourteenth century couple united Switzerland and in so doing, surely saved Western Europe from the entrenchment of a fratricidal enclave to rival the Balkans. This fascinating and compelling story unveils one of the best kept secrets of Catholic Europe and bears a timely message for our tormented age.

152 pages, hardback, £14.95, ISBN 1-901157-76-8

The Saint Austin Press' Titles

THE MONASTIC INSTITUTES   *St John Cassian*

This is the first complete and unabridged translation into English of this key text from one of the most important masters of the spiritual life. Cassian's teaching underlies that of St Philip Neri and St Francis de Sales and was also one of the major influences on St. Benedict.

Cassian had experienced monastic life in Egypt in the ancient desert tradition. He was ordained deacon by St John Chrysostom, but ended life in Marseilles where he had founded two monasteries. He wrote this practical treatise at the request of a French bishop who was seeking guidelines on the monastic life.

The work is divided into two sections, both of which are full of practical and hopeful advice for the living of the Christian life. The first part, "On the Training of a Monk", relates many of Cassian's fascinating first hand experiences of the tradition of the Desert Fathers. He makes suggestions as to how their spirit can be reapplied in a Western, more urban context.

In the second part, "The Eight Deadly Sins", Cassian sees the classic weaknesses of the human condition as obstacles or hurdles in the Christian life, which the spiritual athlete - under grace - can conquer one by one on the road to sanctity.

The translator, Fr. Jerome Bertram F.S.A., is a priest of the Oxford Oratory.